SIR WALTER GILBEY SERIES

# THE HARNESS HORSE

OTHER BOOKS AVAILABLE
By Sir Walter Gilbey

*Farm Stock of Old*

*Concise History of the Shire Horse*

*Sport in the Olden Time (Cockfighting)*

Barouche Horses, 16.2 to 17 hands.

FIFTH EDITION

# *The Harness Horse*

BY

SIR WALTER GILBEY, Bart

REVISED BY

SANDERS WATNEY

*President of the British Driving Society*
*Past President of the Coaching Club*

Foreword by Walter Gilbey

**THE SPUR PUBLICATIONS COMPANY**
Hill Brow, Liss, Hampshire, GU33 7PU

ISBN 0 904558 21 5



Photoset by Petaprint, Petersfield
Printed and bound in Great Britain by
Redwood Burn Limited, Trowbridge & Esher
for the Publishers:
THE SPUR PUBLICATIONS COMPANY,
Hill Brow, Liss, Hampshire, GU33 7PU

# CONTENTS



## LIST OF ILLUSTRATIONS

## FOREWORD TO THE FIFTH EDITION

It is a great pleasure to have been asked to write the foreword to this revised edition of *The Harness Horse,* which my Grandfather wrote at the end of the last century.

I should like to congratulate The Spur Publications Company and their Directors, Dr. and Mrs. Batty, on their enterprise and initiative in reprinting not only this book by my Grandfather, but also so far three of his other books: *The Shire Horse, Farm Stock of Old,* and *Sport in the Olden Time.* I feel it is a great tribute to their author that some three-quarters of a century after they were written, these books are still in wide demand, and giving pleasure to many readers. I look forward to assisting The Spur Publications Company in any way I can with the reprint of other books, which my Grandfather wrote.

I am most grateful to my friend, Mr. Sanders Watney, for so kindly agreeing to my request to update *The Harness Horse* from the turn of the century to the present day. There are few people in the horse world, who have such an intimate and practical knowledge of, or who have done so much for, carriage horses and driving as Mr. Watney. As founder of the British Driving Society in 1954 and its President for many years, he has taken a leading part in re-establishing driving and carriage horses in the British Isles. He and Mrs. Watney have also written several books and many articles on all aspects of driving and like my late Father, the second Sir Walter Gilbey, Bt., are great believers that everything connected with horses should be done properly. Mr. Watney has also done a great deal to re-establish coaching, as Vice-President of the Coaching Club from 1956 to 1968 and President from 1968 to 1975. For many years he regularly drove the famous Watney coaching team to the Red Rover Coach at shows, and also exercised them every morning before going to work. I am delighted that Pinto, a piebald gelding, for many years driven by Mr. Watney, is now with the Gilbey Horses on the Isle of Man.

With the Gilbey Horses, my wife and I are maintaining our family connection with carriage horses, which was started by my Great-grandfather, who was thc owner driver of a stage coach, the 'Cambridge Fly':

and carried on by my Grandfather and late Father, my late Godfather, Mr. Sebastian Gilbey, and the late Captain Frank Gilbey, whom Mr. Watney mentions as a co-founder of the British Driving Society. In the summer the Gilbey Horses are on display to holiday makers, who visit the Isle of Man—rightly called the Gem of God's earth—as well as being driven by my wife and me, while in the winter we hunt them with the Isle of Man Bloodhounds. As will be seen from the picture of them, which the publishers have kindly used as a front cover for this edition and also the illustration in Chapter 8, they are all 16.1½ to 16.3 hunter type bay geldings. I am also glad to say that they are all born and bred in the British Isles.

Thus I have a great personal interest in my Grandfather's original message that the British Isles should once more become the world centre for the breeding of carriage horses.

Walter Gilbey.
Ballacallin Moar,
Marown,
Isle of Man.

CHAPTER 1

# *A Survey in 1904**

## WANT OF CARRIAGE HORSES IN ENGLAND

It cannot be denied that we as a nation devote our attention almost exclusively to the breeding of horses for sport. Having indulged to the full our preference for race-horses and riding-horses, we have hitherto rendered ourselves almost completely dependent upon Continental breeders for our supplies of high-class harness horses.

It will no doubt surprise many people when they are told that those beautiful match pairs of carriage horses, standing from 15.2 to 16.2, and the good-looking teams in private coaches which were among the greatest attractions of our West-end streets and fashionable resorts in the London season, were not the English horses they fondly believed them to be; they were, with few exceptions, importations from the breeding centres of France, Germany, Hungary, Austria, Italy and Holland.

---

*Written by Sir Walter in 1904 but amended to past tense in the interest of clarity.

The grand-looking bays and dark browns with which the Royal and Vice-regal stables were stocked were not the English or Irish bred horses we would preferably associate with British royalty, but were, a large proportion at all events, importations from abroad. The same applies with equal truth to the animals with which the state carriages of our city magnates were horsed.

Enterprising and self-denying as our French neighbours have been in their exertions to obtain the best of our breeding stock to supply their military requirements, there was necessarily a limit to the price the Republic could pay her home breeders for young animals; and the French authorities viewed with impatience and dislike the trade which had been forced upon British dealers in high-class harness horses by the paucity of suitable animals in England.

In course of his most interesting and instructive evidence before the Lords' Commision on Horses in 1873 (popularly known as "Lord Rosebery's Commission"), Colonel Conolly, Military Attache to the Embassy in Paris, said that the remount officers in France "complain very much of all their best Norman horses going to England for carriage horses. They say directly there is a good promising young horse or mare, it is sure to go off to England." The special superiority of the Anglo-Norman breed will be noticed on a future page.

## LONDON DEALERS PURCHASE ABROAD

English dealers who made a speciality of horses for harness and general road use went abroad in search of the animals they required, knowing perfectly well that upstanding carriage horses, possessed of shape and action, were to be found in the breeding centres of the Continent. They then brought them back to their stables in London until buyers came along.

Enterprising London dealers had, in America and Canada, as well as in the countries mentioned on a previous page, their agents ever on the outlook for good-looking animals suitable for carriage use and for road work in London and other large cities.

It is important to note the evidence

given by the two largest jobmasters in London before the *Royal Commission on Irish Horse Breeding,* in 1897. Mr. Henry Withers, referring to a period ten to twelve years before the Commission said, "We went abroad a great deal and for four or five years we had one buyer in Lexington and another in New York."

Mr Withers proceeded to say, "We do not want to go to America or to go abroad if we could buy in England or Ireland, but American horses at that time were very dear. I remember buying ten horses that just came off the boat at Liverpool, and gave £110 apiece for them. The week before last I went from London to Hanover, where I bought six horses; from there I went to Brussels; from Brussels I went to Ghent, where I bought four; from there I went to Lille. I went to Paris, where I saw a large quantity of horses. I bought two."

Mr. Wimbush, in course of his evidence, stated that he began to go to Normandy for horses about ten years previously. "The horses there were very large, 15.3 or 15.2, and occasionally up to 16 hands; but they are horses of beautiful appearance, very handsome,

LANDAU HORSES, 15.3 to 16 hands.

and splendid goers, they not only step well, but go most excellently on their hind legs."

Had the Commissioners made enquiry into the breeding of these "splendid goers," they would have discovered how large a part the Hackney had played in establishing the breed of Anglo-Norman carriage horses.

## FOREIGN HORSES COMING TO ENGLAND

The growth of our dependence on foreign countries for horses of the useful type has been dealt with at length elsewhere.* It will be sufficient to mention here that in the ten years, 1863-1872, we bought 29,131 horses, while in the ten years, 1893-1902, we bought 340,337 horses from foreign breeders. A proportion of these—the most valuable proportion if the smallest—consists of high-class carriage horses.

---

**Horse Breeding in England and Horses for the Army*. By Sir Walter Gilbey, Bart. Vinton and Co., Ltd., 1904.

BREEDING STOCK SOLD TO FOREIGNERS

America secured one of the horses to which all the best trotting blood in the United States is traced, in the year 1788, when *Messenger* was exported; and in 1822 another sire, *Roger Jary's Bellfounder* (55) out of *Velocity* by *Stevens' Bellfounder* by Moot's famous horse *Pretender,* was landed in Boston. *Pretender* was a dark brown horse, standing 15.2; his first notable performance was to trot two miles in 5 minutes 54 seconds, under a heavy weight on grass.

His son *Stevens' Bellfounder* was matched to trot sixteen miles in an hour, carrying 14 stone on the road. *Velocity* was also a marvellous trotter; and thus *Jary's Bellfounder* had in his veins the best blood in Norfolk; at five years old he trotted nine miles in 29 minutes 38 seconds. The blood of both *Messenger* and *Jary's Bellfounder,* is found in *Rysdyk's Hambletonian*

CHAPTER 2

# *Carriage Horses*

## HOW TO BREED CARRIAGE HORSES

A good Hackney stallion is the best horse in the world. It is not extreme speed at the gallop or trot which makes either a good harness horse or the horse required for military purposes; it is staying power, strength, activity, quickness of perception, and docility; and all these qualities are as prominent in the Hackney as swiftness is in the thoroughbred horse. He has been tried on his merits; and on their merits alone, without enquiry into descent or pedigree, we paid high prices for his progeny sent over to us as carriage horses.

The most valuable of the carriage horses received by us from the United States and Canada descend from the Hackney sires purchased in England. Breeders in both countries have learned the value of this strain of blood, and have been buyers of English Hackney sires for more than 100 years.

Fortunately for ourselves we still

possess in our several breeds of horses material that cannot be equalled by those of any country in the world; we still possess the very best of the old Hackney breeding stock, and though it is as yet more remarkable for quality than quantity its numerical strength increases yearly, under the fostering care of the Hackney Horse Society.

It is not, surely, too much to ask breeders to admit that the horses got in England by Hackneys from judiciously chosen mares are likely to be at least as good as horses got by Hackneys in France or Hungary? The breeding grounds of those countries are not superior to ours, nor do they possess any great climatic advantages over those of England.

Granting, therefore, that our opportunities are at least equal to those of our Continental neighbours, we can, without fear of challlenge, assert that on the Hackney sire we must rely to breed the stock of which we stand in greatest need, namely, high-class upstanding carriage horses.

## MARES SUITABLE TO BREED FROM

It goes without saying that the Hackney sire must be used with discrimination and judgment; but if mated with sizeable mares of his own breed, with thoroughbred mares, with hunter mares possessed of size and substance, or with the big mares called in the trade *vanners* and having thoroughbred blood in their veins, his stock can be depended on to supply the class of animal we want.

Writing to the *Field* in June, 1896, Mr. Alexander Morton gave a striking instance of the good results obtained by using a Hackney sire on an Irish mare.

He said:—

"A neighbour of mine bought a clean-boned clever Irish mare, one of the sort so common in Ireland that do not come to weight for a hunter, and are sold as this one was for about 25 gs. He had four gets from her by different thoroughbred horses, each of which was sold at four years old for less than £40. He then put her to a Hackney sire, and the first produce was sold at over £80. Another neighbour, Mr. Scott, of Carluke, bought a light Irish mare for about £20. She was by *Ascetic,* and turned out too small for the hunting field. This mare he crossed with a Hackney sire, and the first produce is one of the best mares now in the country—No. 3856 *Gilly-flower,* sold at Mr. Scott's sale for 150 gs., champion of all ages at the great Cardiff Show last year, and now valued by her owner at nothing short of four figures.

## FAILURE IN PRODUCING CARRIAGE HORSES

When it was thought that railways would take the place of coach-horses and post-horses, we almost ceased to breed them. This was a mistake which English breeders have never corrected: the old market for coach and post-horses is of course gone for ever; but there is still considerable demand within this country for high class harness horses. No stamp of horses sells more readily or brings a better price than a good up-standing carriage horse with shape and action.

Increased prosperity due to the spread of railways, the discovery of gold in our colonies and many other causes, raised the general standard of living; and where one man kept carriage horses in early Victorian days, twenty or twenty-five kept them in 1904.

Our failure to breed such animals has been due to disinclination rather than inability. Thanks to the endeavours of the Hackney Horse Society, more attention has been devoted to the breeding of this our finest carriage horse over a long period: and the export certificates granted by the society show that the discerning foreign buyer is quite as anxious to possess the best of our Hackney stallions and mares as he it to purchase our best thoroughbred and other pedigree stock.

In producing cattle, sheep and pigs, English breeders stand pre-eminent, and the nations of the world depend upon us for their foundation stock, and for the fresh blood needed to improve and raise the standard of their herds and flocks. Ever since the time of Robert Bakewell, who made so conspicuous a mark on the annals of stock-breeding between 1775 and 1800.

Englishmen of the stamp of Bates, Booth and Torr have displayed marked judgment in their endeavours to establish distinct varieties of cattle, sheep, and pigs; and their successes remain to bear witness to the soundness of their methods.

Among cattle we have now the Shorthorn, Hereford, Polled Angus, Devon, Sussex, Kerry, Jersey, Guernsey, and others, each variety perfectly distinct in appearance; among sheep we find equally distinct breeds developed to the same standard of perfection; and again the same evidence of judicious selection in the case of the pig.

## WANT OF SYSTEM IN BREEDING CARRIAGE HORSES

The Carriage horse of high class stood alone among domestic animals as the one we could not produce at home in numbers sufficient for our requirements. The haphazard method of breeding which was far too common in England was likely to produce horses fit for use in any sphere but in harness.

Mr. E. Greene, M.P. (now Sir Edward Greene, Bart.), made the following pregnant statement in course of the evidence he gave before the Lords' Horse Breeding Commission in 1873:

> "I think that harness horses are really the most scarce animals; that is to say, a carriage horse, a phaeton horse or a horse to drive in a dog-cart. The qualifications for a hunter are not of the same description. With a hunter men put up with a good deal. A horse that will jump is called a hunter, and people manage to find horses in that way; but for a harness horse you want a certain amount of power and shape to fill the eye and they are very difficult to get."

The English breeder's choice of a sire almost inevitably fell on a thoroughbred horse if one was available, and the thoroughbred had not the trotting action necessary in a harness horse; he was bred to gallop, not to trot, and his progeny will resemble him. Sir Edward Greene said in reply to a question put by Lord Rosebery that unless the thoroughbred get a hunter, "the horse he gets is not a horse of great value from lack of action . . . . nothing is so valuable as a horse that steps well and that a thoroughbred does not often get. "

CHAPTER 3

# *Movement*

## TROTTING *v*. GALLOPING ACTION

The action of the horse at the trot differs widely from the action at the gallop; and when it becomes necessary to perform a long journey, which requires the horse to travel on several successive days, the trot is the pace on which dependence must be placed.

This was clearly understood in the sixteenth century, as witness the law of Henry VIII, referred to in Chapter 7: to attempt the accomplishment of a long journey at the gallop would obviously bring the horse to an early standstill. We have bred to secure these paces in their highest perfection, and having established distinct breeds, each as perfect for its purpose as is humanly possible, we must measure each by its appropriate standard of merit.

William Cavendish, Duke of Newcastle, put this point in simple language in a work published by Thomas Melbourne in the year 1667. His Grace was a great authority on equine matters in his day, and we cannot do better than quote him

Victoria Horses, 15.1 to 16 hands.

on the subject. "On the perfect shape of a horse," he said, "in a word I will show you the ridiculousness of setting down the perfect shape of a dog! A mastiff is not a greyhound; nor a greyhound a Lancashire hound; nor a Lancashire hound a Little Beagle; and yet all very fine dogs of their kind."

Precisely: the English race-horse, hunter, and cart-horse are "all very fine horses in their kind," because with each we have for generations taken the utmost pains to develop it and breed it true to type; but we have left it to the foreigner to supply us with high-class harness-horses, and he has shown us that it is equally possible to produce the upstanding carriage horses we have neglected for our own requirements.

## SHAPE AND ACTION OF CARRIAGE HORSES

The pictures of Barouche, Landau, Victoria and other horses for harness given in these pages were drawn from life. In each of the animals portrayed there is a preponderance of Hackney blood.

To describe a perfect animal in writing is impossible; the attributes which go to secure the essential qualifications of the horse for active road work are beyond the power of pen to record, and can only be appreciated in the moving animal by men conversant with those qualifications.

To say that the breeder's aim should be to produce the most valuable animal is to state a general proposition whose soundness no one will deny; and despite the unsatisfactoriness of verbal description it may be desirable to sketch the outline of the *perfect* carriage horse.

He should be upstanding; the neck springing well from the shoulders, which should be deep and well set back into the loins; back not too short or cob-like; ribs well arched ; hind-quarters *broad* and muscular; and tail set high. In harness he must bend, or in other words, wear himself gaily, and be full of fire and animation; he must move with true, direct, and pliable shoulder and knee-action in front, and with freedom behind.

## HORSES CAN BE BRED FOR ALL PURPOSES

It is well known among breeders, not only of the horse but of any animal, that continued endeavour to develop and perpetuate one particular quality, while it results in greater perfection of that sought characteristic, is always accompanied by manifest deterioration in other attributes.

Take the thoroughbred race-horse, for example; during the past 150 years he has been bred purely for racing. This was not always so. In the old *Sporting Magazine* of 1821 we find reproduced from the painting by George Stubbs, R.A., a portrait of *Mambrino* (who was got by *Engineer,* by *Sampson* by *Blaze* by *Flying Childers*), and an account of him from which the following extracts are taken:

> "Mambrino belonged to a peculiar class or variety of the English race-horse . . . he was master of the highest weights over the road or field, and was never beaten on the turf till the edge of his speed was blunted by the severe labours of constant exercise and running. He beat all the best horses of his day at their own play, going too fast for the speedy and running too long for the stout . . . As a stallion [he was] more calculated to get hacks, hunters and coach horses, than racers. He, however, got a number of middling racers and some good brood mares, but no runner of the first or even second class. He went in remarkably good *trotting* form, and we have heard that he would have trotted fourteen miles in one hour."

It is worth knowing thus much about *Mambrino,* because this horse was the sire of *Messenger,* who was exported to the United States in 1788. *Messenger* was the ancestor on the sire's side of *Rysdyk's Hambletonian,* who on the dam's side owned *Jary's Bellfounder,* a Hackney, as his grandsire; and *Hambletonian* was the "King of American trotting sires."

## GALLOPING POWER OF THE RACE-HORSE

To bring to their perfection the galloping powers of the race-horse it was necessary to devote attention entirely to that pace; and the result of directing attention exclusively to *speed* has been the sacrifice to some extent of such qualities as action and stamina. For generations now we have bred for speed and speed only, with the perfectly natural consequence that the qualities which are not primarily essential to a successful turf career have to a very great extent disappeared.

Coach or Post Horses, 15.3 hands.

## TO BREED HORSES ACCORDING TO REQUIREMENTS OF MAN

It goes without saying that horses can be bred as required to fulfil the wishes and requirements of man. In this country the blood of the thoroughbred has been sought and used as though swift movement at the *gallop* on the turf and that alone were the only essentials; in America the decendants of *Messenger* and the Norfolk-bred *Jary's Bellfounder* have been carefully cultivated to ensure the highest speed on the *trotting* track, other qualifications being ignored as completely as in England for the development of the one remunerative quality. Nothing else is to be expected; the great value of the stakes offered for racing and trotting naturally compels studious endeavour to breed only such horses as shall be likely to win money.

The thoroughbred sire is the only animal from which to breed race-horses; his inherent galloping action and speed are so implanted in him by in-breeding during nearly two hundred years that the typical race-horse in England is as rarely suitable to beget stock for general purposes as is the American trotting sire.

Let it not be supposed for one moment that it is sought to disparage the English race-horse or the American trotter for the purpose for which each respectively has been produced with such infinite care; but it is necessary to lay stress on the car dinal point of view, namely, that successful endeavour to develop one and only one quality involves the depreciation of other qualities as a natural consequence.

## NO SCARCITY OF MARES IN ENGLAND

It was a common cry that for years many of our best mares have been bought up by the foreigner; but there are plenty left in this country for breeding purposes; and it only remains to mate them properly. It is true that the Continental buyer has purchased mares in preference to geldings; and in exercising this preference the Continental buyer has shown his longer sightedness.

For immediate use, for the direct purpose as a saddle or harness animal, the mare is quite as useful as a gelding and, while costing no more, has the further value to which the foreign purchaser with his thrifty instincts is fully alive; the mare is used to breed from when her career of active service is at an end, whereas the value of the gelding when past work is neither more nor less that the knacker is pleased to set upon his carcase.

## PREJUDICE AGAINST MARES

There has long been a strong prejudice in England against mares for harness, the result being that mares could be purchased at a lower price than geldings; a fact, in conjunction with the advantage already indicated, which has not been without its influence on the Continental buyer.

From the earlier part of the nineteenth century, when, as "The Druid" tells us, the Norfolk Hackney had an "almost European reputation," horses of this breed have been in keen demand on the Continent, more especially among the breeders of France and Oldenbourg.

From around the year 1870 to 1904 the effect of the Continental demand for roadster breeding stock has been more keenly felt than ever, owing to the fact that foreign buyers have materially raised the standard of their requirements.

Mr. J. East, of the well-known firm of Phillips & East, in giving evidence before the Lord's Commission on Horses in 1873, said of the French agents: "They buy the very best and they get mares; you cannot get them to buy a bad mare." They did not confine their purchases to any particular breed of mares: roomy hunting mares and mares of that class were eagerly purchased to cross with Hackney sires.

As with the mares so with the stallions. All the experts examined before that Commission agreed that the foreign buyers outbid the English for animals of good class, sparing neither pains nor money to secure them.

The late Mr. H. R. Phillips informed the Commission that his firm sent "from thirty to forty every year of those roadster stallions to France and Italy and different countries. They sent as many as they could procure." When asked how the number of Hackney stallions reported at that date compared with the number reported ten or fifteen years previously (say about the year 1858), Mr. Phillips stated that "The number has not increased because they (the foreigners) have always taken as many as they could get.

### THE SUCCESS OF FOREIGNERS IN BREEDING

For many years the Government of the Republic controlled, in a great measure, the breeding operations of the country. Responding to necessity the French authorities set themselves the task of ascertaining how the animal most serviceable for France as a nation could be produced; and, having settled this point adopted and steadily pursued the policy which has resulted in giving the French the horse most suitable for military purposes; in other words, the ideal cavalry horse bred on the lines of our hunters, and best horse for the road and artillery work. In France these animals have to a large extent been developed by the introduction of the Hackney stallion.

CHAPTER 4

# *Paris in 1904*

## PARIS HORSE SHOWS

At the horse shows in Paris the exhibits surpassed those of any other country. The show was held every year and remained open for two weeks; it took place in the year 1904 in the large exhibition building in the Champs Elysees (Gran Palais), and it would be difficult to describe the excellence of the classes or the practical character of the competitive tests.

The animals shown consisted of young horses from different breeding centres of France. The competitions included jumping over fences, and more formidable obstacles were not to be seen in any showring in the world; there also were driving competitions for single horses, pairs, and teams, and displays of military evolutions by young cavalry officers.

The interest taken by the Parisians in the show was not less remarkable than the merit of the show itself. Every day brought thousands of visitors, who paid not less than 5 francs (20p) for admission. The writer was informed that the average sum taken daily at the gate was upwards of

£2,000.

The enthusiasm displayed by the people of Paris can be compared only to that which distinguishes the attendance at the Dublin Horse Show, where the visitor sees the best collection of animals for sport and pleasure in the kingdom.

The noteworthy difference between the great Irish Show and that of Paris, however, was the fact that while Dublin caters primarily for the hunter, the French capital organised a show at which horses suitable for the nation's requirements, cavalry, artillery and road horses were assembled. It was this *national* character which lent the Paris show its great importance and rendered the public interest therein so commendable and impressive.

## THE ANGLO-NORMAN BREED

The success of the French in establishing a breed of road-horses from a foundation of Hackney blood was nowhere more noteworthy than in Normandy. So marked were the pre-eminent merits of the animals bred in that Province, that they were known on the Continent as the Anglo-

Norman* breed; and the Government agents of Austria, Hungary, and other Continental nations visited Normandy to purchase the stallions of that breed.

Surely these facts compel the reflection that we possessed the best materials to work upon; we had the "foundation stock" and its possession should have stimulated our endeavours to maintain the historical reputation of Great Britain as a breeding ground of the best horses in the world.

## THE CONTINENTAL POLICY

The discriminating intelligence the foreigner displayed in making his purchases from us was the keynote of his whole policy as a breeder; his success in developing a superior class of roadster was due to the judgment and selective skill he had brought to bear upon the vital matter of mating and line breeding.

By constant attention to the principles of mating, he produced animals true to type; in fact, established a breed whose conform-

---

*Anglo-Norman is a cross between the English Hackney and the French coaching mares.

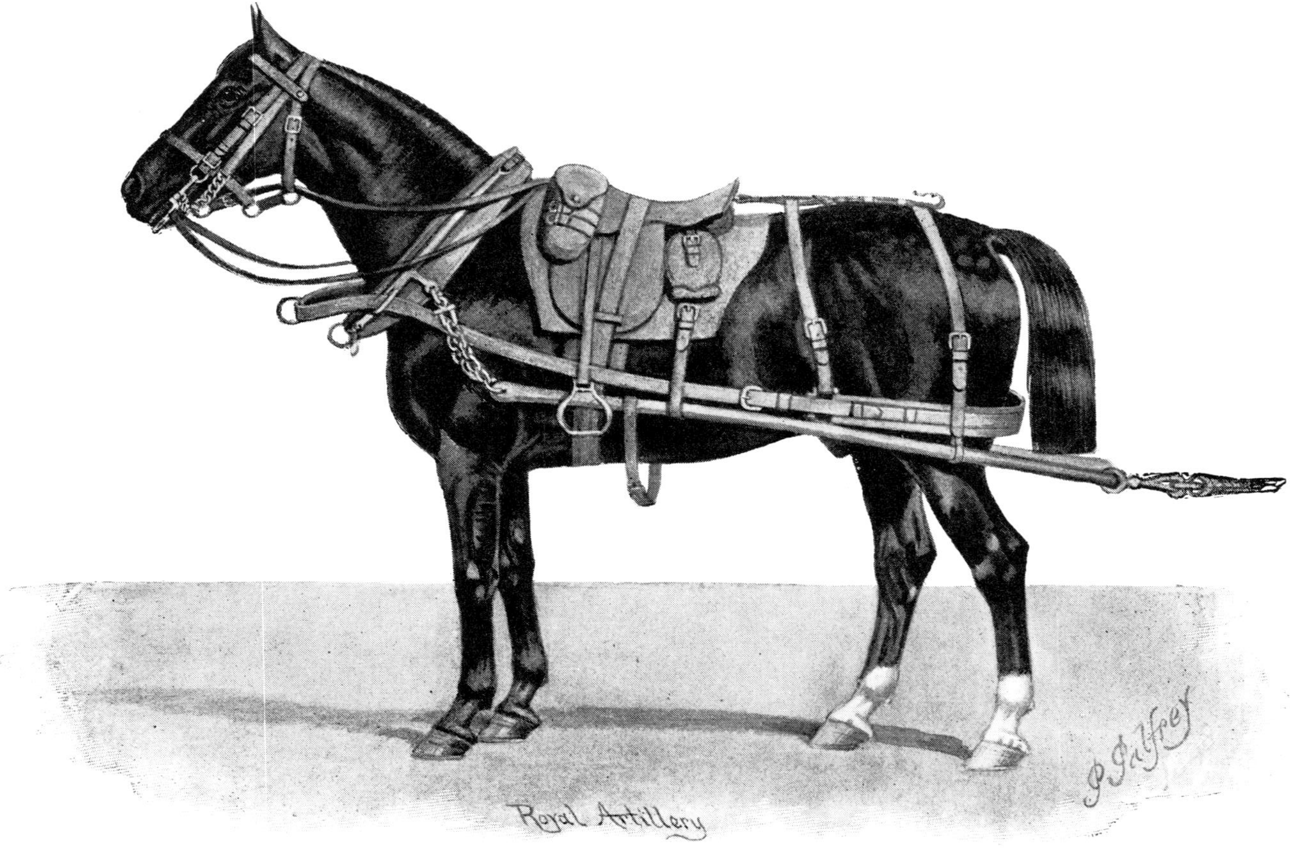

R.H.A. Gun-Team Horse.

ation, grand carriage, and elastic step were constant, to use a breeding term, and which was admittedly superior to the horse bred for the same purpose in Great Britain and Ireland.

Nor have we far to look for the stimulating influence which caused the Continental breeder to devote his attention to the production of horses for road work. We, in our insular security, never felt so keenly as European nations the necessity for supply ing the equine needs of vast armies; and while we have been able to devote ourselves to breeding horses for racing, steeplechasing, and hunting, the Governments of France, Germany, Hungary, Austria and Italy, had, on principle, encouraged the evolution of an animal for road work; a class of horse on which they would depend for cavalry, artillery, transport—in fact, for all military purposes.

## FOREIGN DEMAND FOR HACKNEY SIRES

In 1883, two years before the death of Mr. H. R. Phillips, the writer*

* Sir Walter Gilbey, Bart.

had an interview at Wilton Crescent, Belgrave Square, with that gentleman, who purchased *Phenomenon* to go to Yorkshire. Mr. Phillips then gave the following account of that famous horse and his influence on the Yorkshire breed:—

"The horses in Yorkshire were not good enough for the London trade, and about the year 1838 I purchased from Mr. John Bond, of Cawston, Norfolk, the celebrated sire Phenomenon for Mr. Robert Ramsdale, of Market Weighton, Yorkshire. I reckoned him at that time the best stallion in England. In height about 15 hands 1½ inch, on well-formed, short legs, good feet, deep girth, quarter symetrical, full of courage, with wonderfully all-round true action; and Phenomenon proved a valuable sire, as the Yorkshire mares although sizeable, lacked girth, symmetrical form and action. The stallions in use at that time, in the district of Market Weighton, were very inferior and leggy."

The success of *Phenomenon* in Yorkshire induced Mr. Phillips to recommend his Continental customers to purchase sires of this breed for use in their studs. He sold several horses* got by *Norfolk Cob,* the sire of *Phenomenon,* as stallions to go abroad. "One in particular he remembers he sold to a nobleman in Normandy, which, put upon thoroughbred mares produced remarkable stock." (Hackney Society's Stud Book, vol. 1, *Introduction,* by H. F. Euren).

---

* Among these was Kendle's Norfolk Cob (476), sold in 1845 or 1846.

What measure of success attended this step we may gather from the statement of the late Mr. Hetherington, who was a large buyer of horses for Continental Governments. He stated in his evidence before the Irish Commission on Horse Breeding that he had purchased Hackney stallions for the French *Haras* Department for the last twenty-three years; buying during that period from twenty to upwards of thirty stallions each year.

These Hackney sires were used to procure artillery horses, because "they do not want to canter, and they improve the courage of the native mares." Mr. Hetherington added, "they are very popular with the breeders; they are used in preference to the thoroughbred, and improve their horses more than anything." It would be difficult to furnish more convincing evidence of the merits of the Hackney than this.

The records of the Hackney Horse Society give the numbers of animals of this breed exported every year. They are as follows:—

| Year | Stallions | Mares | Total |
|---|---|---|---|
| 1889 | 189 | 70 | 259 |
| 1890 | 105 | 175 | 280 |

| | | | |
|---|---|---|---|
| 1891 | 189 | 90 | 279 |
| 1892 | 105 | 175 | 280 |
| 1893 | 92 | 92 | 184 |
| 1894 | 42 | 29 | 71 |
| 1895 | 48 | 45 | 93 |
| 1896 | 52 | 30 | 82 |
| 1897 | 60 | 66 | 126 |
| 1898 | 32 | 29 | 61 |
| 1899 | 46 | 33 | 79 |
| 1900 | 60 | 30 | 90 |
| 1901 | 50 | 47 | 97 |
| 1902 | 75 | 49 | 124 |
| 1903 | 104 | 57 | 161 |
| 1904 | 117 | 102 | 219 |

It must be added that by no means every exporter of a Hackney notifies the sale to the Society, and the figures which follow, taken from the summary of Export Certificates granted, do not therefore represent the total number exported in any year.*

The first fact to arrest the eye in glancing over these figures is the heavy falling off in the number of Hackneys exported in the years 1893 and 1894 from those in previous years. The diminution is explained by the action of the American Government, whose Customs Regulations were so altered as to make the importation of Hackneys extremely difficult. The im-

* At the large show of Hackneys held in the Agricultural Hall in March, 1904, there was a brisk demand by foreign buyers in search of stock to ship abroad.

port duty of 33⅓ per cent. *ad valorem* was of itself enough to administer a severe check, but in addition to this it was required that the sire and dam of each parent of every Hackney landed in America must have been registered in the Hackney Horse Society's Book!

Such legislation as this could have but one result on the trade in a breed of horses whose Stud Book had then only been in existence for ten years, the Hackney Horse Society having been founded in 1884. The pedigrees would have been forthcoming in the vast majority of cases if not in all; but certificates of registration were not to be had for the conclusive reason that the animals had lived, and often died, before the Hackney Stud Book existed. These were the registered exports to the United States for the few years preceding and following this Act. They speak for themselves:—

| In | Stallions | Mares | Total |
|---|---|---|---|
| 1890 | 78 | 170 | 248 |
| 1891 | 116 | 79 | 195 |
| 1892 | 78 | 170 | 248 |
| 1893 | 36 | 71 | 107 |
| 1894 | 6 | 14 | 20 |
| 1895 | 11 | 16 | 27 |
| 1896 | 5 | 19 | 24 |
| 1897 | 2 | 6 | 8 |

Mr. Edward T. G. Lindsay, writing on "American Hackneys" in the *Live stock Journal Almanac* of 1895, said:—

"Out of thirty-nine Hackney stallions exhibited at the Great Madison Square Garden Horse Show, New York, in November, 1893, twenty-nine were bred in England, and of the fifty-four Hackney mares (which do not include those in the half-bred classes) forty-six also came from the old country, and they won all the awards with the exception of four animals, which had a look in with their English rivals in the two-year-old and yearling classes."

The classes for mares and geldings by registered Hackneys out of unregistered mares, we are told by the same writer, "clearly demonstrated what good Hackney stallions are capable of doing when crossed with native mares."

The falling off in exports during the period 1898-1901, shown earlier, needs no explanation. The Hackney breeding industry, like all other industries, felt the influence of the South African War.

Examination of these export certificates shows that the Hackney sire was gaining ground in Buenos Ayres and South Africa, and in those years the Japanese had been steady purchasers in pursuance of the scheme organised by the Mikado's Government in 1900 to improve the local breed of horses. Austria and Italy, it goes without saying, were regular purchasers of pedigree stock in England.

CHAPTER 5

# *Demand for Horses*

## THE MARKET FOR CARRIAGE HORSES

Even when regarded as a business, we can hardly be surprised that the breeding of thoroughbreds and hunters should almost monopolise attention; the demand for high-class carriage horses was a town rather than a country demand, and appealed less to the resident in horse-breeding districts; but it was considered that English breeders who reared horses for profit as well as for pleasure should devote more attention to the harness horse? Harness horses were in much greater demand than riding horses; it may fairly be estimated that for one riding horse in use, there were fifty harness horses.

Passing reference has been made to the sums obtained for brougham horses and for match pairs. That the moderate animals worth comparitively small sums in the market formed the majority of stock obtained is a point which should not have been urged as deterrent; and for the reason that this was so largely the result of lack of care in mating. The success of the French gave proof of this.

Given due care in mating, however, there was no reason why a highly remunerative proportion of young stock suitable for the London carriage horse market should not be obtained. Could it be denied that the demand for harness horses of the best stamp was one that was pregnant with opportunity for the breeder who would use the Hackney sire? He had no superior as a getter of road horses, and his claim to be considered as *pure-bred* as the race-horse could not be doubted.

## CHARACTERISTICS OF THE HACKNEY

Let it be borne in mind, too, that the Hackney has more to recommend him than the true action and elegant carriage required of the high-class horse: good temper and graceful manners are peculiarly characteristic of the breed, and he possesses the soundest of constitutions, a quality above all things desirable in an animal which is most liable to exposure under all conditions of weather and is left so greatly to the care of servants.

The Hackney Horse Society's records furnish some telling evidence concerning the soundness of the bred in the shape of statistics, giving the number of horses rejected by the examining veterinary surgeons at the shows held during those years. Prior to 1896 the practise was to subject to veterinary examination only those horses in a class which the judges selected as likely to take the prizes. These are the figures for the half dozen years ended 1895:—

| Exhibition of | Horses Examined | Rejected as Unsound |
|---|---|---|
| 1890 | ... 170 ... | 9 |
| 1891 | ... 116 ... | 4 |
| 1892 | ... 187 ... | 7 |
| 1893 | ... 249 ... | 8 |
| 1894 | ... 217 ... | 13 |
| 1895 | ... 223 ... | 4 |

In 1896 the system was altered and all horses that entered the ring were required to undergo veterinary examination before the judges looked at them. These are the figures for the past nine exhibitions up to 1904:—

| Exhibition of | Horses Examined | Rejected as Unsound |
|---|---|---|
| 1896 | ... 396 ... | 17 |
| 1897 | ... 438 ... | 23 |
| 1898 | ... 436 ... | 21 |
| 1899 | ... 437 ... | 30 |
| 1900 | ... 400 ... | 21 |
| 1901 | ... 406 ... | 24 |
| 1902 | ... 434 ... | 16 |
| 1903 | ... 422 ... | 21 |
| 1904 | ... 416 ... | 24 |

These figures speak for themselves to those whose knowledge of equine matters enables them to appreciate their significance.

The soundness of the modern Hackney is merely one more proof of the results of selective care exercised for generations; for nearly two hundred years the aim of the breeder of this horse has been the development of a robust and hardy constitution.

In the Hackney, therefore, we have shape, action, courage, manners, staying power, and soundness. What would you more?

## PEDIGREE OF THE HACKNEY

Incessant repetition of part of a truth is certain in course of time to elevate the fraction to the dignity of the whole; frequent reiteration of the one fact that our thoroughbreds are descended from a few horses of Eastern origin is therefore likely to obscure the larger fact that our thoroughbreds are not the only descendants of that Eastern stock. The thoroughbreds of to-day trace their descent to the *Byerly Turk* imported in 1689, to the *Darley*

The Darley Arabian (Imported into England 1706.)

*Arabian* imported in 1706, and the Godolphin Arabian imported twenty-four years later.

The term "thoroughbred" was adopted to denote the progeny of these three sires with the Royal Mares, called "King's Mares," imported into England from the East, in the reign of King Charles II.; and it cannot be too often and too closely pressed home upon breeders that in *all Hackney pedigrees* the foundation sire is found to be no other than that same *Darley Arabian* whose blood in the racehorse is the *cachet* of breeding fashion!

There is diversity of opinion as to which one of these three Eastern sires wrought the greatest influence on our breed of horses, and did most towards the establishment of the reputation England has obtained for her thoroughbreds; but there is no question as to the one of the three which was most beautiful in make and shape; and that was the *Darley Arabian*, imported about 1706 from Aleppo, by Mr. Darley. A portrait of this celebrated horse is here given.

*Shales,* the original (699), said Mr. Henry Euren after a painstaking review of the history of this family, was the first noteworthy trotting Hackney Stallion; and concerning *Shales'* ancestry he wrote:—

"There would appear to have been a large proportion of English blood in the dam of *Blaze* (Confederate Filly) though no one can say what was its character—whether running, trotting or ambling. The preponderant element in *Blaze,* however, was Barb and Arab blood, the trotting tendency of which would appear to have mixed freely with, and to have added to that inherent in the 'strong common-bred' dam of the Original Shales' horse. The fact that in the seventh generation from *Blaze* on each side, the reunion of the blood in *Rysdyk's Hambletonian,* the sire of so many fast trotting American horses, should have proved to be of the most impressive character, would appear to warrant the conclusion that there was a strong latent trotting tendency in the near ancestors, on one, if not on both sides of *Blaze*."

*Shales* is mentioned as "the fastest horse" of his day.

With scarcely an exception, the Hackney sires of to-day descend in the direct line from this famous horse. The *Darley Arabian* begat *Flying Childers* (foaled 1715), the speediest race-horse of his time, and considered by many a better horse than *Eclipse*; *Flying Childers* begat *Blaze*; and it was through *Blaze* that the county of Norfolk achieved fame for its breed of Hackneys. *Blaze* (foaled 1733) was the sire of the *Original Shales,* foaled in 1755 out of a Norfolk mare.

*Shales*, so far as is known, had only two sons, *Scots' Shales* and *Driver* (187), the latter out of a mare by *Foxhunter,* by the famous horse *Sampson.*

The directness of the descent of the Hackneys of to-day from the *Darley Arabian* may be most conveniently and clearly shown by setting out the pedigree of the male line of the defunct Hackney sire *Danegelt*:—

The *Darley Arabian*, foaled 1702, begat

*Flying Childers,* foaled 1715, who begat

*Blaze,* foaled 1733, who begat

*Shales* (the original, 699), foaled 1755, who begat

*Driver* (187), foaled 1765, who begat

*Fireaway* (*Jenkinson's,* 201), foaled 1780, who begat

*Fireaway* (West's, 203), foaled 1800, who begat

*Fireaway* (Burgess', 208), foaled 1815, who begat

*Wildfire* (R. Ramsdale's, 864), foaled 1827, who begat

*Phenomenon* (P. Ramsdale's. 573), foaled 1835, who begat

*Performer* (Taylor's 550), foaled 1840, who begat

*Sir Charles* (Beal's, 768), foaled 1843, who begat

*Denmark* (Bourdas's, 177), foaled 1862, who begat

*Danegelt** (174), *foaled* 1879, *died* 1894.

If remoteness of ancestry be held proof of purity of blood in equine as in human families, the Hackney must take precedence of the modern race-horse, for the Hackney has in his veins the blood of the old English race-horse, tracing his descent from animals which ran on the English Turf at a period when the great grandsires of the Darley and Godolphin Arabians were yet unfoaled.

The original *Shales,* as already said, was the grandson, through *Blaze,* of *Flying Childers* (foaled 1715), the fastest race-horse on the turf of his time. The pedigree of many of the best race-horses now living traces back to *Flying Childers.*

## PROPER HEIGHT FOR A HACKNEY STALLION

The type and stoutness of the Original *Shales* has been transmitted through his descendants to the best Hackneys of the present time. What this type was we shall

---

**Danegelt* was sold in 1890 for £5,000, to join the Elsenham Stud.

learn on a later page from the writings of Richard Blome. The true type of old-fashioned Hackney came near being lost at one period, and no doubt it would be spoiled, if not lost altogether, were breeders to use large stallions over 15.2, which are not of the true Hackney type.

The true type is a horse not exceeding 15 hands 2 inches in height. The writer well remembers a visit he paid to Norfolk in 1863 in search of animals large enough to make carriage horses. The only harness horses to be found in those days were called "Norfolk Cobs," and cobs they were in size as well as in name, standing about 14.2 to 14.3.

Two hundred years ago, and later, good saddle-horses for road work were in general request, and great attention was paid to the breed. With the increase and improvement of roads and coaches, saddle-horses gradually went out of general use, and the breeding of Hackneys was neglected.

The demand from the Continent for Hackney blood grew up and, increasing as time passed, helped to promote decay, as the foreign buyers made a point of purchasing the best of the stock that remained. Very few of the old-fashioned type

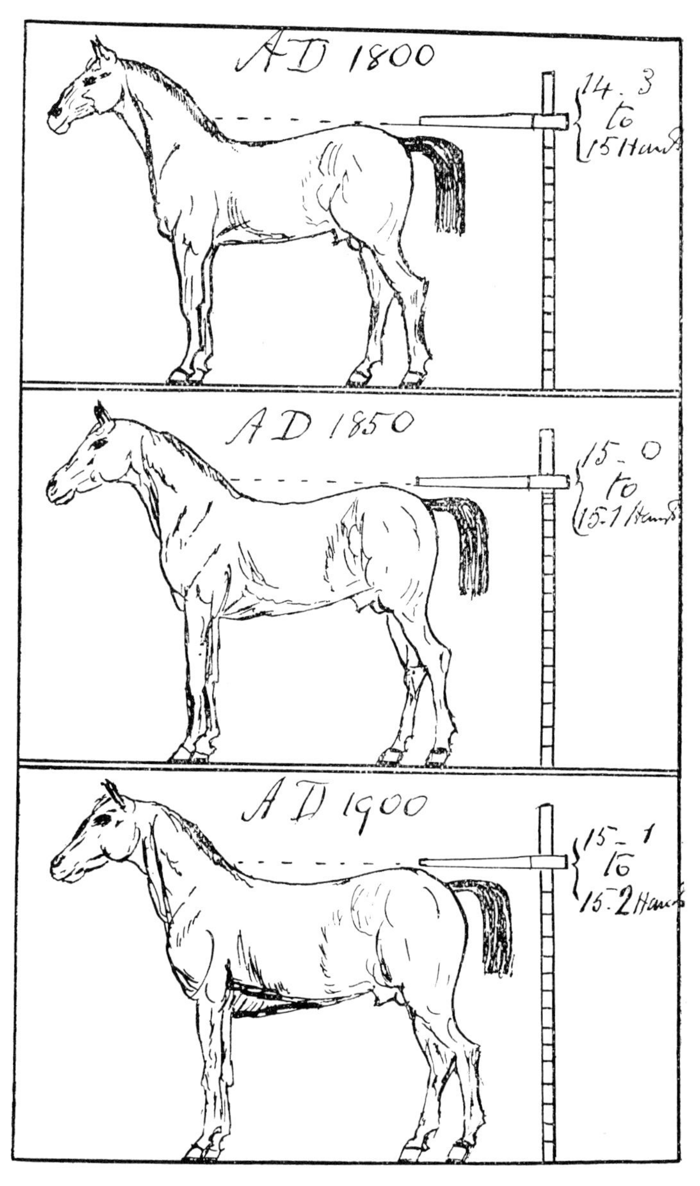


THE HACKNEY IN 1800, 1850 AND 1900.

were left us, and of these *Performer* and *Phenomenon* were the best.

It was fortunate, indeed, that this valuable remnant was left, for when the saddle-horse went out of general use, the Norfolk breeders made no attempt to keep their Hackney stock up to the standard accepted as the best in Richard Blome's time.

From the remnant of the old breed, represented by such horses as *Performer* and *Phenomenon*, modern Hackney breeders have succeeded in grading up the old English Hackney strain to 15.1 or 15.2; and the 15.1 to 15.2 sire may be accepted as the best to produce carriage horses.

Carriage horses may be bred to any size by judicious selection of mares; they may be "vanners," weight-carrying hunter mares, or roomy thoroughbreds. Such crosses will produce horses of from 15.3 to 17 hands 1 inch, for which there is a great and regular demand.

CHAPTER 6

# *Horses for Travel*

## SADDLE HORSES IN THE PAST

All travelling was performed on horseback until about the year 1564, when the first "long waggons" began to ply between London and large provicial towns.

There were no roads, and therefore, while rude carts were employed in agriculture, all merchandise was carried on pack-horses, strings of which continued to traverse the country for many years after a regular system of stage coaches catered for travellers. Nor did the coach do away with the use of the saddle-horse by able-bodied men.

Only a few of the main highroads of the kingdom were fairly good: most were indifferent if not exceedingly bad, and the cross-roads were the most wretched tracks imaginable even in George III's time, and furnished good reason for using powerful horses for the heavy stage or post carriage.

## THE TERM "HACKNEY HORSE"

This term, derived from the French *hacquenee,* was brought into use in England by the Normans. It originally applied to a saddle-horse of good stamp, lighter and more active than the Great Horse used by armour-clad knights.

There is a record* of the "horses of the bannerets, knights, esquires, and vallets of king's household," which were killed at the battle of Falkirk in the year 1298; this roll of horses killed in the battle was prepared so that the owners or their relatives might be awarded compensation for their loss; and it includes numerous "hackneys."

The animal so called was used by persons of high rank; in the *Privy Purse Expenses of Princess Elizabeth of York,* under date September 11, 1481, we find particulars of "2 yards of purple velvet cloth of gold for the covering of a saddle for a person of astate, and an harness in velvet cloth of gold for an hackney." Indeed, the words hackney and palfrey would seem, for a long period of history, to have been equally applicable to the best

---

*Bain's *Calendar of Documents Relating to Scotland.*

saddle-horses.

The hackney being the saddle-horse, men who hired out horses for journeys were called "Hackney men"; thus in process of time the name came to signify a hired horse, and we have evidence that the "Hackney man," or job master, kept an exceedingly good stamp of animal.

The word "Hackney" having come to mean a horse that could be hired, by one of those curious perversions of language brought about by popular usage,* it was applied to means of conveyance, other than horses, that could be hired, and thus in 1605 we hear for the first time of "hackney" coaches, and in 1634 of "hackney" chairs.†

## ROADSTERS OF THE COACHING PERIOD

In the early coaching and posting days, as has been shown in the preceding pages,

---

*A good example of this suggests itself in the word "collie," which originally meant a sheep; dogs used by shepherds being called "collie dogs," *i.e.*, "sheep dogs," in time became known as "collies"; whence what was properly the name of a sheep is now become that of a dog.

†*Early Carriages and Roads*, by Sir Walter Gilbey, Bart. (Vinton and Co., Ltd., 1903.)

the roadster was an absolute necessity; and universal and continuous demand naturally produced on the spot a supply of horses in which soundness of constitution and limb, speed and endurance were indispensable.

In no part of England was more attention paid to these horses than in the Eastern counties. It is thought that Norfolk, Suffolk and Yorkshire owe something of the merit of their trotting horses to early importations of Norwegian stock by the Danes.

Mr. H. F. Euren in the able *Introduction* he contributed to volume i. of the Hackney Horse Society's Stud Book, said "the fact that the trotting horse was in the last century [1701-1800] found most plentifully in those districts of the kingdom where Danish settlers had left their indelible marks of occupation and habitation, warrants the assumption that to Norse horse stock they in great measure owe their characteristic action."

However this may be, the fact remains that past history of the Norfolk and Yorkshire breeds is full of passages reflecting their merits. Mr. H. R. Phillips, in his evidence before the Lords' Committee on Horses in 1873, says: "The Hackney is a class of itself. We date them back from Mr. Theobald's *'Old Champion,'* which cost 1,000 guineas." This horse, registered under the name of his breeder as *'Champion, Hewison's,'* was foaled in 1836; he was by *Bond's Norfolk Phenomenon,* and is described as a bay with black legs, standing 15.3.

In earlier days of Mr. H. H. Dixon ("The Druid"), when the Norfolk Hackneys were grown scarce, that authority wrote (*"Post and Paddock,"* 1856): "About a quarter of a century since Norfolk had an almost European fame for its strong-made, short-legged hackneys, which could walk five miles an hour and trot at the rate of twenty. *Fireaway, Marshland, Shales,* and *The Norfolk Cob* were locomotive giants in those days, and the latter was the sire of *Bond's Norfolk Phenomenon,* 15.2, who was sold to go into Yorkshire in the year 1836, and afterwards went to Scotland when he had seen his twentieth summer, and astonished his canny admirers by trotting two miles in six minutes. Those now left are descended from these breeds, but as they arrive at maturity they are sold to go to France."

The writer goes on to remark that "Four

or five very good hackney sires are still in the county, and among them Baxter's red roan, *Performer,* 15.3, foaled 1850, for which 500 guineas is said to have been refused. The chestnut, *Jackson's Prickwillow,* 15.2, and a son of his, *Prickwillow,* out of a very noted mare belonging to Mr. Charles Cooke, of Licham, which is said never to have been 'out-stepped,' is also highly spoken of. Mr. Wright, of Tring, has a bay, *Shales,* 16 hands, foaled 1851, with rare action; and a black 14.2 cob, foaled in 1852, of Mr. Baldwin's has earned a much more worthy mention than we can give him by winning the first hackney stallion prize at the last Norfolk Agricultural Show. Lord Hastings has two hackney stallions of the Fireaway breed, which are occasionally seen in harness."

A grand example of the Norfolk Hackney at this period was *Hazard,* a cabriolet horse belonging to Lord Chesterfield. The symmetrical shape and bold action of this horse is well shown in the portrait here reproduced. *Hazard* could trot at the rate of sixteen miles an hour, and when put up for sale at Tattersall's in 1836 was purchashed for 330 guineas by the Marquis of Abercorn.

The famous *Paston Letters* contain evidence concerning the trotters which were obtainable in Norfolk in the fifteenth century. Records show that in the seventeenth century Norfolk had a reputation for its roadsters; for Marshall, in his *Rural Economy of Norfolk,* published in 1795, said that before Queen Anne's reign (1702-1714) the farmers of the country used an active breed of horses which could not only trot, but gallop; and the curious team-races this writer described, proved that the Norfolk breed of the seventeenth and eighteenth centuries was sure-footed as well as active. The team consisted of five horses which were harnessed to an empty waggon; thus Marshall speaks as an eye-witness:—

"A team following another upon a common broke into a gallop, and, unmindful of the ruts, hollow cavities and rugged ways, contended strenuously for the lead, while the foremost team strove as eagerly to keep it. Both were going at full gallop, as fast indeed as horses in harness could go for a considerable distance, the drivers standing upright in their respective waggons."

Laurence, in his Treatise on the Horse, says of the Suffolk and Norfolk horses:—

"I have seen a cart horse of this description which, bating a little coarseness of the head, was perhaps as fit to get hacks and hunters from proper mares as the best horse alive. I have also heard of a Norfolk farmer, who about fifty years ago [*i.e.,* 1750]

Lord Chesterfield's Norfolk Hackney, Hazard.

[or thereabout], had a peculiar sort which he styled his Brazil breed. This blade of a farmer it seems would unharness one of his plough horses, ride him to a neighbouring fair, and after winning with him a leather plate, ride him home again in triumph to his wife."

There can be no doubt but that the Norfolk Hackney traces his descent on the dam's side to this breed; his pedigree on the male side has already been described.

## DISAPPEARANCE OF THE SADDLE-HORSE

From the time that stage and hackney coaches became numerous, the saddle-horse gradually fell into disuse for ordinary travel, though farmers and others whose vocation compelled frequent journeys over rough tracks and on roads along which coaches could not ply, continued until the earlier years of the nineteenth century to ride as their forefathers had done.

With the saddle-horse went the pack-horse, which was now replaced as a carrier of goods by the canal boat, the waggon and the carrier's cart.

The change was necessarily very slow. In the year 1673 one John Cressel wrote a pamphlet, *The Grand Concern of England Explained,* wherein he complained of the harm wrought by the stage coaches.* He declared since these had been set up "there is not the fourth part of saddle-horses either bred or kept in England that there was before," and that there would be again if the coaches were suppressed. In 1731 Dean Swift wrote to his friend, Mr, Gay, rebuking him for his preference for travelling by coach; the letter clearly indicates that it was then still usual for country gentlemen of active habit to ride rather than use the stage coach.

There was sound reason for the man to whom time was a consideration to prefer the saddle to the coach. The earliest roads for wheel traffic very commonly ran along the dry beds of streams and old water courses; rough tracks in dry weather and veritable quagmires in wet seasons. They also followed the rough bridle paths which ran over the hills, where firm ground had led the traveller on horseback and the chapman or pedlar, with his train of pack-horses to select their route.

---

*We must not associate the vehicles of this period with those of the brief "golden age" of coaching. These early stage coaches were cumbrous, heavy, springless carriages, drawn by heavy horses and travelled, as a rule, at a pace of not more than four or five miles an hour.

The general adoption of Macadam's system of road making in 1819, together with Telford's engineering feats, resulting in hard, smooth highways free from steep gradients, introduced the "golden age" of fast coaching, which did much to give journeying in the saddle its final blow. And it will be right to say that during the period 1650-1820, the breeding of saddle-horses was by slow degrees given up in favour of the production of coach-horses, for which demand was growing up. It is significant that in the numerous works on stock breeding and agriculture in Britain, which appeared during the period 1775 - 1800, exceedingly little is said concerning the breeding of horses for the saddle. The saddle-horses of Yorkshire and Norfolk are the principal breeds referred to by the agricultural writers of that period.

When railways became established and it was recognised that the coaching era was at its close, there prevailed a strong feeling that harness horses would no longer be required; and this belief, combined with the depression in agriculture at the period between 1835 and 1845, led the farmers to abandon horse-breeding to a great extent.

CHAPTER 7

# *Historical Records*

## ANCIENT WRITERS ON THE HACKNEY

In the works of old writers, and also in the laws and royal proclamations, of the middle ages, there is frequent mention of "trotting" horses and geldings, which were, in fact, hackneys, the word "trotting" being employed to distinguish the animals from "ambling" horses.

In the early days when long journeys were made in the saddle, persons of rank were much addicted to the use of horses which had been taught by artificial means the gait known as ambling; the amble, as Ralph Holinshed tells us in the edition of his *Chronicles* published 1585, was much easier and more agreeable to the rider than the trot. Writing of English horses, Holinshed says:—

> "Such as serve for the saddle are commonly gelded and are now grown to be very dear among us, especially if they be well coloured, justly limmed [well shaped], and have hitherto an easy ambling pace. For our countrymen seeking their ease . . . . . delight very much in these qualities, but chiefly in their excellent pace . . . . . it is moreover very pleasant and delectable in his [the rider's] ears in that the noise of their well-proportioned pace doth yield comfortable sound as he travelleth by the way."

Trotting horses, however, were considered more serviceable than amblers. Blundeville, whose book on horsemanship was first published in 1558, says: "It is not meet for divers respects that horses for service [war] should amble." Hence the obligation imposed by the Statute 33 of Henry VIII, c. 5, which was made in 1542, upon persons of various degrees to keep stallions of the trotting breed.

Every Archbishop and Duke was compelled by this Act to "have, find, sustain and maintain," seven stoned trotting horses for the saddle, each horse to be three years old and upwards and at least 14 hands in height. Every marquis, earl and wealthy bishop, was to keep five such trotter stallions; other bishops, viscounts and wealthy barons, were obliged to keep three; less wealthy persons two; and every layman who wore a silk gown, or whose wife wore "any French hood or bonnet of velvet," with any of certain specified articles of jewelry, was obliged to keep one stoned trotting horse for the saddle.

The wording of this law is notable, as it indicates recognition of the trotting horse as a distinct breed; it ordains that maintenance of "cart horses and sumpter horses" shall not be reckoned compliance with its provisions, these being animals of different and inferior types.

It is both interesting and significant to find that, long before Henry VIII's Act to encourage the breeding of trotters was placed on the Statute Book, trotting horses were held in particular esteem in Norfolk, the county with which the Hackney has always been identified.

One of the famous *Paston Letters,* written in 1470, makes mention of "one of Berney's horses," for which 20 marks, or £3 16s. 8d. was demanded and for which "not a penny less would be taken." The Berneys of Norfolk were a good county family, and the value set upon this trotting horse may be measured by the fact that eight years earlier, in 1462, Lord Howard paid only £1 16s. 8d. for a "grey nag to send to the French King," as a gift.

Margaret Paston, writing to her husband Sir John, about the year 1465, from their home at Haylesdon, near Norwich, said: "There be bought for you three horses at Saint Faith's fair, and all be trotters, right fair horses, God save them, and they be well keeped." St. Faith's, which is about three miles from the county town, was long famous for its annual stock fair.

Thomas Blundeville, who lived at New-

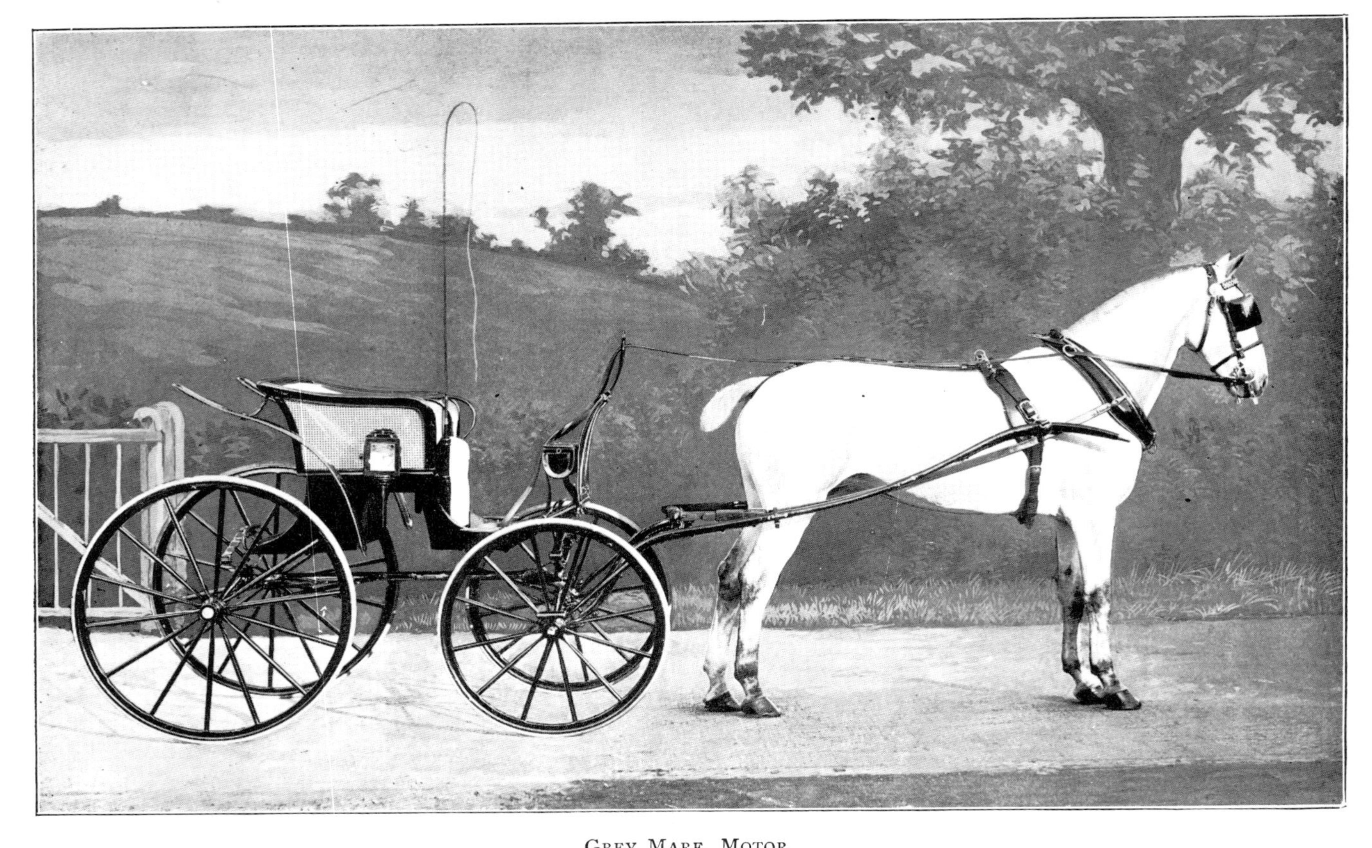

GREY MARE, MOTOR.
Sire Crown Derby, registered in Hackney Stud Book, Volume X.
Crown Derby is by Lord Derby II.

ton Flotman in Norfolk, also bears witness to the merits of the local breed of horses in his time—the 16th century.

He said:—

"I have known some carriers that go with carts, to be so exquisite in their choice of horses as, unless thay had been as comely to the eye as good in their work, they would not buy them, insomuch as I have seen sometimes drawing in their carts better proportioned horses than I have known to be finely kept in stables, as jewels for the saddle."

Nearly a hundred and fifty years after Henry VIII's act to foster the breed of trotting horses or hackneys was placed on the Statute Book, Richard Blome, in his *Gentleman's Recreation* ("Printed by S. Rotcroft, dwelling at the upper end of *Dutchy Lane* near *Somerset House* in the *Strand,* 1686"), instructs his readers how to choose stallions to breed such horses:—

"If you would breed for the Road, make choice of a good strong *Hunter*, that has naturally good *Legs* and *Feet*, a short *Back* and good *Quarters*, and let him be one that is not of a Skittish or Stubborn Temper: or if you are curious [particular] and would have very fine *Padds*, you may take the same measures which I told you before the *Manage*, only Geld your *Colts* and when you break them, if they take it well, let them be taught to *Amble*."

Of the Mare he says:

"If you would breed for the *Race* and *Hunting*, your mares must be lighter [than for breeding Road horses], with short *Backs* and long *Sides*; their *Legs* must be something longer and their *Breasts* not so broad, and always make choice of such as you are sure have good Blood in their *Veins*."

Breeders "for the Manage" (or *Menage)* are advised that the stallion should "be a *Turk, Barb* or *Spaniard,* one that is good in his kind, and naturally of a docile and gentle temper, though lively, vigorous and bold in actions."

As regards mares, for all purposes, Blome holds that:

> "Certainly none in the World are better to Breed on than our *English*, provided you Suit tham to your particular design; if you would breed for the *Menage* or *Pads*, let your *Mares* have fine *Forehands* with their *Heads* well set on, but not too long *Necks:* broad *Breasts*, large and Sparkling *Eyes*, and great *Bodies*, that their *Foals* may have room enough to lye: with good *Limbs* and *Feet:* let them be of a gentle and good disposition, and their motions naturally nimble and Graceful. In a word, remember always that the more good qualities your *Mares* have the better will your *Colts* generally be."

Fifty years later we have testimony to the excellence of the horses which could be hired from the Hackney man (or job master, for the old term seems to have fallen into disuse before this period) in the writings of a Swiss gentleman, Mons. C. de Saussure, who resided in England from 1725 to 1730. Mons. de Saussure wrote an account of his experiences, a translation of which was published about 1900. He was greatly impressed with the good qualities of the horses which were thus let out for hire.

"They are excellent. When you travel on horseback in England it is always at a trot or a gallop and Englishmen hardly know what it is to go at a foot's pace. Naturally in this way you travel very rapidly. Soon after my arrival in England, wishing to ride to Guildford, which town is thirty miles distant from London, I went to a horse-dealer and told him I wanted to hire a horse for two days. This man told me that if I had no business to keep me at Guildford I could easily return the same day, and he offered me a sorry looking animal that did not look worth two crowns. I expostulated, but he told me to let the horse go; that I was not to press and not to stop it, and that I might be assured I should be satisfied. In truth I got to Guildford early in the day, stopped there a few hours and was back in London at seven in the evening. My horse never stopped going at a hand gallop both there and back, excepting on the stones and on the pavement, and there I had to let him walk, for it would have been impossible to go faster: but as soon as he was on the roads he started off at a gallop without a word from me and required no persuasion either with the whip or spurs. This little episode surprised me, but I did not know then the worth of English horses."

The same writer condemns the London hackney coach as ugly, dirty and badly balanced, but says that "most of the horses are excellent, and fast trotters."

Thus we see at different times the saddle horse used, for road travel was known by different terms. Hackney is the earliest. Dame Paston, in 1470 writes of "trotters"; the Statute of Henry VIII, 33 of 1542, refers to trotting stallions. Hakluyt, in his *Collection of Travels,* published in the year 1600, uses the term "roader" as that in vogue among the colonists of Virginia to describe the saddle horse.

Eighty-six years later, in 1686, Richard Blome in his *Gentleman's Recreation*, writes of "Horses for the Road," and "Padds" or "Pads," to describe the same breed. And at the beginning of the 19th century, Lawrence, in his *History and Delineation of the Horse*, writes of the "Hack, Hackney, Roadster, Road Horse or Chapman's Horse: a cloddy compact horse or gelding of this description is now and then styled a *Cobb*."

CHAPTER 8

# *The Decline*

PERIOD 1904 TO 1914

Although the motor-car had been extensively developed on the Continent during the eighties, Britain, perhaps due to prejudice, was slow to take up this new form of transport, and it was not until the first decade of the new century that the internal combustion engine came into fairly common use in this country. Even so, owing to the adverse legislation, development was slow, but by the outbreak of the first world war in 1914, it was estimated that a quarter of a million mechanical vehicles of all types were on the road in England, and the greater proportion of these were privately owned motor-cars.

The Englishman's natural love of horses and carriages died hard, but die it did when the obvious advantages of the motor-car became apparent. Motoring moreover became a popular sport with many wealthy land owners who had previously been great supporters of the horse and carriage.

The first world war did little to stem the collapse of harness horse breeding, although the policy advocated by Sir

Walter Gilbey was certainly justified. Every moderately young and sound horse was commandeered by the Army and sent overseas—frequently never to return, nor to be replaced. In the early stages of the war, horses and forage were of more value to the country than mechanical vehicles, and petrol for limited commercial and private motoring was possible, but very few horses, except a minimum of breeding stock—principally thoroughbreds, were kept privately. It was, therfore, only due to harness enthusiasts such as Lord Lonsdale, the Marquis of Shrewsbury, and others, that some British harness horse breeds managed to survive—principally those of the Hackney breed, which has always been the back-bone of our harness stock.

## YEARS 1918 TO 1939

Although in the years between the wars there was practically no market for carriage horses as such, the production of mechanical lorries and vans had been slow to revive after the war, and up to the middle thirties there was still a strong demand for vanners, ponies, and cobs for

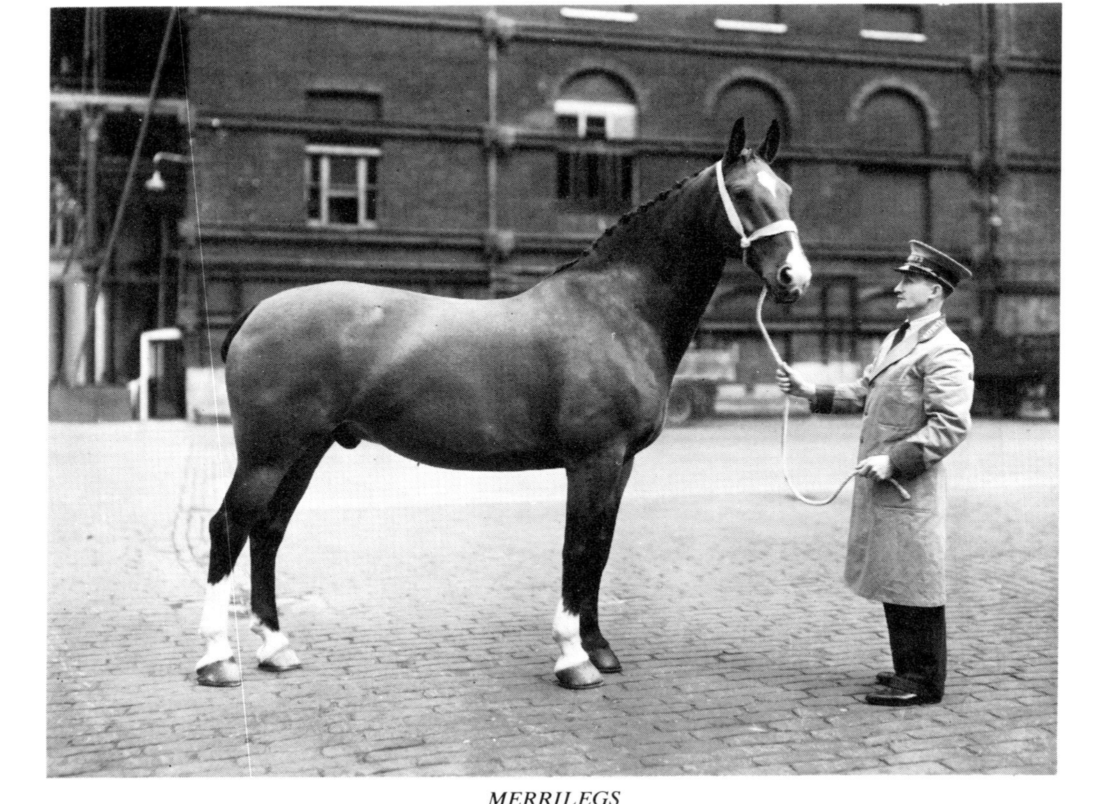

*MERRILEGS*

A good type of Yorkshire Coach horse purchased in 1936 by Mr. S. Watney for Watney, Combe, Reid & Co. Ltd.—a consistent winner in Trade Show classes.

(Photo: W. Rouch)

commercial work—many firms considering that there was great advertising value in the smartly turned-out transport, and they vied with each other in the appearance of their horses and equipment. Many may remember the magnificently matched pairs of Yorkshire coach horses owned by Carrier Charles Wells & Son, Messrs. J. Buchanan & Sons, and Messrs. Schweppes, together with the smart pairs of Hackneys produced by the biscuit manufacturers Meredith & Drew, and caterers J. Lyons & Co., also the splendid Welsh ponies and Hackneys owned in great numbers by the Dairy companies.

All this commercial enterprise was a great boon to breeders, since it provided a useful outlet for animals which did not measure up to top show standards, but when this trade collapsed with the advent of the second world war, it was difficult to imagine how *any* harness horse breeds could survive. Indeed, the Yorkshire Coach horse and Norfolk Hackney never revived, and the only true Harness breeds left in Great Britain were Hackneys and Cleveland Bays.

Although in the years immediately before the first world war the general use of harness horses had decreased, there had been a great upsurge in showing, and well filled classes of harness horses were a feature of all shows—particularly at the International Horse Show, which was staged at Olympia in London. The 'international' flavour was very much a feature, and wealthy Americans, such as Mr. Alfred Vanderbilt and Judge Moore, thought nothing of bringing literally hundreds of horses—both Hackneys and Trotters, from the United States to compete in coaching and other harness events, while Mr. Walter Winans, with Hackneys, American Standardbreds, and Orloff Trotters, was able to make at least one entry in every harness class. British Hackneys were of course well represented by such well-known exhibitors as Mr. W. A. Barron, and two formidable lady whips — Miss Sylvia Brocklebank and Miss Ella Ross, and many others.

In later years, and carrying on after the first war, some superb teams of Hackneys were shown by Mr. Bertram Mills, Mr. Claude Goddard, and Mr. H. J. Colebrook, while Sir Nigel Colman and Mr. Minoprio, to name only two, headed the classes for Hackney horses and ponies in single, tandems, and pairs. The horses used in teams were invariably Hackneys of about 16 hands and of great substance, with magnificent action. Some were bred in England, but many came from overseas — although these were largely the progeny of British exported stock.

The influence of the Heavy cart horse breeds in Harness horses must not be overlooked, and progeny from Shire, Clydesdale, Percheron, and Suffolk mares when put to Thoroughbred or Hackney stallions, frequently produced good harness horses, as well as hunters, or commercial cobs. Cleveland Bays were also, of course, used — mainly for crossing, although purebreds were kept in the Royal Mews, as well as in the few stables where State coaches were still in use.

The Road coaches, which in the years between the wars ran out of London during the summer season, used mainly cross-bred horses which were usually sold (and made good prices), as hunters in October. Cross-bred horses were generally produced out of a common mare by a more aristocratic sire, yet when the reverse happened on the late Sir Dymoke White's estate in Norfolk, and a Percheron colt escaped and served a Thoroughbred mare, the resulting foal eventually became the best horse in the grey team of the "Red Rover" coach!

In the Second World War horses were not required by the Army to any great extent, although at the outbreak of war, Mr. Claude Goddard's magnificent team of chestnut Hackneys were commandeered—presumably for Yeomanry troop horses—for which they must have been most unsuitable.

## POST-WAR DRIVING

During this war, virtually no horse breeding took place, and only with difficulty was a minimum of Cleveland Bay and Hackney blood preserved—thanks to one or two private enthusiasts. After the war there appeared to be no demand for driving horses since people who had used them during the petrol shortage soon reverted to motor transport, and horse-drawn vehicles were relegated to the scrap-heap. There was also practically no demand for horses in commerce or agriculture, as the advent of the five-day week, and consequent high wages for week-end work, made horses uneconomic.

It appeared once again that there could be no future for harness horse breeding; however, the two harness breeds, especially the Hackney, were saved by export. The ravages of war had reduced the horse population practically everywhere, but British stock, which was always considered the best, was now in world-wide demand—particularly for Hackney, and to a lesser degree, Cleveland Bay stock, and this justified the devotion of those few breeders who had struggled so hard to keep the essential lines going during the war.

Harness classes at horse shows were slow to recover, but curiously, those for coaches, which many thought could not survive the war, were among the first harness classes to be revived, and between four and five coaches appeared at the major post-war shows. Classes for Hackney horses and ponies were also included at most of the major shows, and although poorly filled at first, entries soon increased due to the vigorous efforts of the Hackney Horse Society, supported by one or two breeders.

Private Driving seemed however to be

completely dead, and the demand for harness horses other than show Hackneys, virtually non-existent. There was therefore no incentive for stud owners to breed harness horses *other* than Hackneys of top show quality, or of export standard, and even Hackney breeders had the disadvantage of not having an outlet for animals which were not first class.

## HACKNEYS

The Hackneys then bred were almost exclusively for use in the show ring, and judges looked for courage and action—occasionally to the exclusion of all else. Inevitably these characteristics were emphasised by breeders, which caused some people to consider that conformation had been neglected. Be that as it may, the large Hackney horse began to disappear—indeed there was no demand for it—although one or two excellent teams of Hackney coach horses were shown.

The post-war revival of Hackneys owes much of its success to the skill and hard work of two people: Mr. and Mrs. Frank Haydon. At their Hurstwood Stud they

*SOLITUDE*

by *Buckley Courage* out of *Dark Vision*. An unbeaten champion in the show ring, and probably the world's greatest sire of harness horses.

*(Photo: Thomas Fall)*

have succeeded in preserving many of the essential blood lines established by prewar breeders such as John Partington and others. Mrs Cynthia Haydon, as a member of the famous Black family, was brought up with Hackneys and is undoubtedly the finest whip in England—if not the world—having won the major awards at shows on practically every occasion, since the war, while her husband has great knowledge of both breeding and showmanship. Between them they have persuaded many influential owners, both here and overseas, to take up Hackneys, and are primarily responsible for the revived interest in the breed.

Probably the most important post-war Hackney horse stallion was Mr. Frank Haydon's *Solitude*, and on twenty-one occasions since the war, the Supreme Champion Harness horse was either sired by *Solitude,* or traced back to him. Two more important horse stallions were the late Mr. W. T. Barton's *Walton Diplomat* and *Walton Searchlight*—both of which were out of *Solitude* mares.

In the Hackney pony section there is perhaps no stallion quite so outstanding as *Solitude,* but *Oakwell Sir James* and *Highstone Nicholas,* both having won the

Supreme Pony Championship on several occasions, have stamped their progeny with their own quality, and the top ponies in Australia, South Africa, Holland, Italy and Japan, trace back to these two little stallions.

The statistics given below are of interest in showing how exports have been maintained to the present day (figures from 1889 to 1904 are given earlier):

NUMBERS OF HACKNEY HORSES AND PONIES EXPORTED SINCE 1905
as compiled by The Hackney Horse Society

| *Year* | *Numbers* |
|---|---|
| 1905 | 218 |
| 1906 | 259 |
| 1907 | 381 |
| 1908 | 331 |
| 1909 | 184 |
| 1910 | 311 |
| 1911 | 262 |
| 1912 | 219 |
| 1913 | 196 |
| 1914 | 272 |
| 1915 | 93 |
| 1916 | 41 |
| 1917-18 | 110 |
| 1919-20 | 206 |
| 1921-22 | 270 |
| 1924-25 | 98 |
| 1926-27 | 74 |
| 1933 | 208 |
| 1938 | 131 |
| 1948 | 65 |
| 1954 | 100 |
| 1960 | 84 |

| | |
|---|---|
| 1965 | 96 |
| 1968 | 75 |
| 1971 | 73 |
| 1975 | 114 |

During the period, 1,293 Hackneys were exported to the U.S.A.; 754 to Canada; and 581 to Holland, but horses and ponies were exported in smaller numbers to all Eurpean and South American countries, as well as to Australia, New Zealand, South Africa, Egypt, and Japan.

## CLEVELAND BAYS

Before the first world war, there was a demand in Europe and the U.S. for Cleveland Bays—either pure, or part-bred—for use with State coaches and carriages. These were invariably geldings, with no white markings on them, but many pure-bred stallions were exported to America and the Colonies in order to up-grade the native stock. In the years between the wars, the export demand for harness horses of this type inevitably declined, although there was still a call for Cleveland blood for crossing, and a number of mares as well as stallions were exported to the U.S.A. for this purpose.

After the second world war, the breed really seemed in danger of extinction—despite some export of stallions to improve stock in the U.S.A., Japan, Pakistan, Australia, Czechoslovakia, and Canada. By 1950, breeding in England was almost at a standstill, and in 1960 there were only *three* mature stallions left, and it was only due to the loyalty of one or two enthusiasts who had bred them for years, that the Cleveland Bay was preserved. A few conservative farmers defied the march of progress and continued to keep one or two Cleveland mares which, apart from breeding, could do light farm work, go in harness, and even provide a day's hunting.

This breed received a great stimulus when it was announced that two Olympic show-jumpers, *North Flight* and *Madison Time,* had been sired by Messrs, Keenleyside's *Lord Fairfax* (1946)—one of the few remaining Cleveland stallions in 1962.

It appears that the breed has turned the corner since in 1976 there were now more than thirty stallions at stud in Great Britain, while horses with Cleveland Bay blood are in demand for hunting, show jumping, and eventing—both under saddle, as well as harness.

*Overleaf*

Mr. Walter Gilbey driving the Gilbey Horses as a team at the London Harness Horse Parade in the mid 1960's. This Parade resulted from the amalgamation of the Van Horse Parade with the Cart Horse Parade, of which one of the co-founders was Mr. Gilbey's Grandfather, the 1st Sir Walter Gilbey, Bt., the original author of this book. Following in his Grandfather's and Father's tradition Mr. Walter Gilbey has been President of the Harness Horse Parade and serves on its Committee. Beside him on the exercising brake is Mrs. Gilbey who is an accomplished four in hand whip.

*MR. WALTER GILBEY*
*Grandson of Sir Walter Gilbey, Bart., driving a team of hunters*

CHAPTER 9

# *A Revival*

## FORMATION OF BRITISH DRIVING SOCIETY

The coronation of Her Majesty Queen Elizabeth II took place in 1953, and as befitted the ceremony for a Sovereign so interested in all aspects of the horse, the procession consisted almost exclusively of horse-drawn carriages. The President of the Coaching Club, the late Colonel Arthur Main, with the help of the late Captain Frank Gilbey, organised that members of the Coaching Club should volunteer to supply their horses and to drive landaus in the procession. These were occupied by Commonwealth Heads of State, and Captain Gilbey had the honour of acting as coachman to the late Sir Winston Churchill.

The display of horse-drawn vehicles proved of such appeal to the public, that an enthusiasm for driving was revived. The following year, the Royal Agricultural Society's Show was staged in Windsor Great Park, and an extensive pageant of historic horse-drawn transport—mostly driven by amateurs, was presented daily in the grand ring. This again caught the imagination of the public, and Colonel Main and Captain Gilbey, together with Mr. R. A. Brown, and Mr. Sanders Watney, evolved the idea of forming a Driving Society—in order to assist and instruct anyone interested in driving, before the technique was lost to posterity by the passing of time. Mr. A. Wyndham Brown, the well known harness expert and journalist, gave useful publicity to the proposal, but few people visualised more than between 100-200 members joining, and no one foresaw that within twenty years, the British Driving Society would consist of over 2,000 members, and be under the patronage of H.R.H. the Duke of Edinburgh.

As a result of this renewed interest in driving, classes for amateur whips became popular and well-filled features at many shows. More important, the B.D.S. appointed Area Commissioners who organised non-competitive "meets" throughout the country, and these were well attended by members—particularly those who did not aspire to top show standards, yet enjoyed the sport of driving.

All these activities gave a fillip to the breeders of harness animals, and a market for Hackney horses and ponies—to be used

*H.R.H. THE DUKE OF EDINBURGH*
driving a pair of Cleveland Bays.

*(Photo: Leslie Lane)* *Courtesy: H.R.H. The Duke of Edinburgh*

for *road work,* as well as purely for showing and breeding purposes, was once again in existence. In addition, although animals of all sizes were used, there appeared to be a preference for cobs and ponies, and many breeders of Mountain and Moorland ponies, who had for some years concentrated on *riding,* now found an increasing demand for driving ponies—with the emphasis on those from Wales—particularly the Welsh cob which, traditionally, has always been a strong, courageous, and active harness animal.

## COMBINED DRIVING

In 1971, the F.E.I. (Federation Equestre Internationale), under the Presidency of His Royal Highness The Duke of Edinburgh, drew up rules for Three-Day Event driving for pairs and teams in International competitions. This sport, which consists of a combination of Presentation, Dressage, Cross-country, and Obstacle driving tests, had been practised on the Continent for many years, but was new in England, and encouraged by His Royal Highness—himself no mean exponent of the art—British whips took it up and were soon able to compete with foreign teams with considerable success.

This latest development produced yet another outlet for British harness horses for although foreign breeds such as Gelderlanders, Oldenbourgs, Lipizzaners, and Swedish breeds have been used, the Duke of Edinburgh has competed very successfully when driving a team of Cleveland Bays in Combined Driving events. Hackneys, too, have been well represented in this sport—Mrs. Haydon having been selected a member of the British team which won a Gold Medal at the World Driving Championships held at Munster in 1972. The greatest success in this field however has been achieved by the Welsh Cobs driven by Mr. George Bowman, who were not only in the team to win a Gold Medal at Frauenfeld in 1974, but were also awarded the individual Bronze.

It thus appears that the breeds which at one time appeared in danger of extinction through lack of demand, have been saved once again, and that driving may continue as a popular sport.

## ORGANISATIONS DEALING WITH HARNESS HORSES

| | |
|---|---|
| *British Driving Society:* | *Sec.* Mrs. P. Candler<br>10, Marley Avenue,<br>New Milton, Hants. |
| *British Horse Society*<br>*Combined Driving Committee:* | National Equestrian Centre,<br>Kenilworth, Warwickshire,<br>CV8 2LR |
| *Cleveland Bay Horse Society:* | J. F. Stephenson, Esq.,<br>M.A. (Cantab.),<br>York Livestock Centre,<br>Murton, York YO1 3UF. |
| *Dales Pony Society:* | G. H. Hudson, Esq.,<br>Ivy House Farm,<br>Yarm-on-Leer, Yorks. |
| *Dartmoor Pony Society:* | D. W. J. O'Brien, Esq.,<br>Chelwood Farm, Nutley,<br>Uckfield, Sussex. |
| *Exmoor Pony Society:* | Mrs. J. Watts,<br>Quarry Cottage,<br>Sampford Brett,<br>Williton, Somerset. |
| *Fell Pony Society:* | Miss P. Crossland,<br>Packway, Windermere,<br>Westmorland. |
| *Hackney Horse Society:* | National Equestrian Centre,<br>Kenilworth,<br>Warwickshire, CV8 2LR. |
| *Highland Pony Society:* | J. McIldowie, Esq.,<br>Dunblane, Perthshire. |
| *Hunters Improvement Society:* | G. W. Evans, Esq.,<br>National Westminster Bank<br>Chambers,<br>8,Market Square,<br>Westerham, Kent. |

| | |
|---|---|
| *London Harness Horse Society:* (Inc. London Van Horse, and London Cart Horse Societies) | R. A. Brown, Esq., O.B.E., 65, Medfield Street, Roehampton, London SW15 |
| *New Forest Pony Society:* | Miss D. Macnair, Beacon Corner, Burley, Hants |
| *Shetland Pony Society:* | D. M. Patterson, Esq., 8, Whinfield Road, Montrose, Angus. |
| *Weatherby & Sons:* | 41, Portman Square, London W1. |
| *Welsh Pony & Cob Society:* | T. E. Roberts, Esq., 32, North Parade, Aberystwyth, Cardiganshire. |

HEAVY HORSE BREEDS

| | |
|---|---|
| *British Percheron Horse Society:* | *Sec.* A. E. Vyse, Esq., Owen Webb House, Gresham Road, Cambridge. |
| *Clydesdale Horse Society:* | *Sec.* S. Gilmore, Esq., 24, Beresford Terrace, Ayr. |
| *Shire Horse Society:* | *Sec.* R. W. Bird, Esq., East of England Showground, Alwalton, Peterborough PE2 0XE. |
| *Suffolk Horse Society:* | c/o Church Street, Woodbridge, |

Mr. Sanders Watney, the author, would like to express his gratitude to Mr. Frank Haydon and The Hackney Horse Society, and to Miss Ruth Kitching of the Cleveland Bay Society, for their help regarding these two breeds.